D1524223

Praise for Secrets of the 7th Day

"*Secrets of the Seventh Day* is a practical how-to for Jews and non-Jews alike. It has easy to use skills, recipes, and practices that anyone can easily implement into their life. I warmly recommend it to the busy person seeking a respite from life's frantic pace with the hope that more people will find the peace and deep connection they yearn for. The benefits for anyone for wishing for more time for family bonds, physical rest, and spiritual rejuvenation after a busy week will become apparent when you apply this wonderful advice."

–Rabbi Zalman Schachter-Shalomi

"Sabbath keeping just may be the secret 'fountain of youth, peace, and prosperity' that each of us is walking around in search of! I, for one, crave the peace that Sara Schley presents to us in this small and delightful book, so much that reading her simple words brought me to tears. And rather than making us feel guilty for not having such a practice in our lives, Sara, frees us to be open to the peace that is simply waiting for us. This book is a breath of fresh air in the midst of a suffocating world!"

–The Rev. Dr. Barbara J. Campbell, Pastor,
St. Mark Presbyterian Church, Portland, Oregon

"I read your book in one sitting last Thursday; it is a lovely, generous, inspiring work. I was so touched by it that I brought it up in a conversation with my wife and daughter in the car, and Katie, who is 15, said, 'Why don't we do that?' My hope is that now she will read it and that she will become an advocate for some kind of practice along these lines."

–Rev.Bob Massie, Executive Director, New Economics Institute

Secrets of the 7th Day

Secrets of the 7th Day

How Everyone Can Find Renewal through the
Wisdom and Practices of the Sabbath

Sara Schley

White Cloud Press titles may be purchased for educational, business, or sales promotional use. For information, please write:

Special Market Department
Confluence Books
PO Box 3400, Ashland, OR 97520
Website: www.whitecloudpress.com

Cover and interior design by C Book Services
Photos by Marsia Shuron Harris, motherturtlemusic@gmail.com

Printed in the United States of America

14 15 16 17 18   10 9 8 7 6 5 4 3 2 1

Library of Congress Cataloging-in-Publication Data

Schley, Sara.
 Secrets of the 7th day : how everyone can find renewal through the wisdom and practices of the Sabbath / by Sara Schley.
     p. cm.
 Includes bibliographical references and index.
 ISBN 978-1-940468-18-1 (pbk. : alk. paper)
 1. Sabbath. I. Title.
 BM685.S25 2014
 296.4'1--dc23
                              2014024066

Contents

Foreword

On our second date, I introduced the man, who would become the love of my life, to Shabbat. I explained to him how during this sacred time, I didn't get anything done, but instead directed my attention to simple pleasures, to relationships and to the miracles of Creation. As we lit the candles, blessed the wine and entered in to the secrets of the seventh day, I watched this gentle man fall in love...not with me, that came later...but with the practice of Shabbat.

"I've looked for this all my life," he confided. "I've tried my whole life to carve out some sacred time, but it has always felt like a struggle." Witnessing his process of awakening to the secrets of the seventh day, rekindled my own enthusiasm and appreciation for Shabbat. I watched his body relax, his heart open, his mind expand and his spirit soar. Freed from the slaveries of ambition, guilt, drudgery, compulsivity and habit, my beloved opened to the Divine as a flower to the sun. And our marriage blossomed in the light of Shabbat.

And now, as I read Sara Schley's magnificent book, I am inspired all over again, knowing that her powerful message will relax so many tense bodies, open so many hearts, expand so many minds and set so many souls soaring.

The secrets you are about to receive have the power to effect a radical renewal of body, heart, mind and soul. Here is a message that we have all been longing to hear. Here is the secret: You *are enough*. Your essential nature is good enough, smart enough, beautiful enough. You have enough and you are enough in this very moment. As we lean into this essential truth and let go of our constant struggle, we re-embrace our love of Life itself. We remember as Rabbi Abraham Heschel said, that, "Just to be is holy."

Informed by the fullness of *being*, our life of *doing* is transformed.

Sometimes I call Shabbat, "The Sanctification of Pleasure." On Shabbat I get to slow down enough to fully enjoy the simple pleasures of being alive. The message of Shabbat is to enjoy each breath, each fragrance, each taste, each step. This enjoyment becomes the cure for addiction and over-consumption… because when I can really enjoy this one bite, I don't need to keep eating. On Shabbat I am filled; I am fulfilled. And then I take the message of Shabbat, that sense of fulfillment, into my week.

In every word of this book I sense the presence of an extraordinary messenger.

Sara Schley has a very large vision—nothing less than the transformation of this planet into a place where all life thrives. She has worked for over two decades in multi-national business, non-profit, government and academic sectors; creating, designing, facilitating, teaching and coaching leadership programs and culture change initiatives for a sustainable world.

And yet that expansive vision is expressed most clearly through the small daily details of a life-well-lived. She knows that each of us must take on the responsibility to be the microcosm of this whole wide world. We must attain our own sanity in order to become healers of this crazy world.

Sara is an extraordinary messenger because she is living the promise of Shabbat; she knows the healing power of its spaciousness; she has tasted its sweetness. And she knows how to guide us patiently and compassionately towards the pleasures that call us all, and the wisdom that beats within our own hearts.

The Secrets of the Seventh Day shows us a pathway to sanity…for ourselves and for the world.

Rabbi Shefa Gold is a leader in Aleph: Alliance for Jewish Renewal and is the director of C-DEEP: The Center for Devotional, Energy and Ecstatic Practice. Rabbi Gold is the author of *Torah Journeys: The Inner Path to the Promised Land* and *In The Fever of Love: An Illumination of the Song of Songs.*

A Crazed and Hectic Friday Afternoon

It is Friday afternoon and the deadlines are looming. My third grader, Sam, is getting off the bus at 3:15 p.m. and if I don't meet him, they'll take him back to school. I have to get him and then drive to fetch his twin sister, who goes to a different school 45 minutes in the opposite direction. There are 136 new emails in my inbox and another 55 flagged as urgent. My to-do list is down to 11 items, but each could be a half-day project.

The twins' birthday is next month and I want to book the public skating rink. I left a message, but haven't heard back. The vacuum's busted again and our lab's yellow hair is covering the purple rug. Outside the living room is a mountain of clean laundry that needs to be folded. The kids' school papers are strewn all over the kitchen counter. Which one of the twins has a field trip next week? Whoever it is needs a swimsuit and a signed permission slip. Sam's school librarian left a voicemail: "Will you be donating books and volunteering at the book fair again this year?"

In two weeks I'm teaching my "Leaders for a New Climate" workshop at MIT. It's a new one that I've created with a trusted and wonderful colleague. His standards are high, as are the expectations of the participants and the venue, so I want it to be impeccable. There are PowerPoint presentations to prepare, agendas to review, and marketing outreach to be done. On the heels of that is my Dad's 90th birthday. My sister-in-law is preparing a tribute for him and has asked each of us to write our fondest memories. My Dad, a gritty, relentless, ambitious immigrants' son drilled his hard-driving manifesto into each of his four children. His anthem, "Work, work, work, think later," etched irrevocably into our characters. During my race to the bus at the moment, I can't think of any fond memories. But I will.

It's 2:15 p.m., one hour before I have to pick up the kids. I've been so busy all day I forgot to eat lunch. My blood sugar's down to my knees, my throat's desert dry, and my nerves are frying. I grab a hunk of peanut butter and an apple for a snack on the fly and notice the "experiments" in the fridge. Experiments as in "science experiments"—my term for the penicillin-like mold growing all over our leftovers from last weekend. As I'm scraping green hummus by hand into the compost, I grumble to myself, "How come Joe never notices the moldy food?" I notice the answering machine is blinking so I hit the play button. It's Susan, sounding a bit annoyed.

"Sara, I left a message with Joe last night asking you guys to confirm about the party this weekend. Didn't hear back from you—can you give me a call, please?"

"Dammit Joe," I'm thinking. "Why is it so hard to write down a message? The paper and pen are right next to the phone!"

The PB and apple make me feel a bit more grounded. We're expecting guests for dinner tonight, so I turn the oven to 425°. Luckily for me, it's one of those ovens that you can time to shut off by itself, so I won't burn the house down. I wash two chickens from our neighbor's farm and pat them dry. I dice red potatoes, chop two onions, and mince ten cloves of garlic, which I add to olive oil and soy sauce. I cut two lemons in half and squeeze two halves over the chickens and stick the the remaining two halves inside the chicken cavities. I shake some rosemary over the whole thing and slide the birds into the oven.

It's 3:07 p.m. Eleven minutes until the bus comes. Back to the office now with my apron still on. Luckily I have no Skype teleconferences this afternoon. Which of the emails have to be answered? I don't even try to check Facebook. Never liked it anyway—I prefer live friends to electronic ones.

I grew up in the 1960s before voicemail, email, cell phones, Internet, Facebook, Google, twitter, fax machines, answering machines, texts, smart phones, iPods and iPads permeated every aspect of our lives. How did we survive? I was raised in a culture where there was so little correspondence in any given day that the expectation was that you would respond to all mail and phone calls. The pace was human. I've internalized the standard that it's polite and honorable to get right back to people who contact me. But now the exponential growth of high-speed electrons traveling to my in box makes that impossible. No one can do it. But my inner Martha Stewart wants me to.

It's exhausting. I can't do it all! Yet I still aspire to. June Cleaver, meet Carly Fiorina, meet Hillary Clinton, here I come.

3:15 p.m. and the emails are still flying in. I can stretch it to 3:18 p.m. and still make the bus. Time for one more reply.

I throw a leash on the dog (he hasn't been out since morning) and race up the hill. Our driveway rises at a 45-degree angle for 200 yards, and I arrive breathless just as the bus pulls up with Sam. All smiles and 9-year-old enthusiasm about his day.

"Mom, can you grab my backpack?" he asks, tossing it at me. "I want to run down the hill!"

Maybe I can fire off the answers to my MIT colleague's inquiries before we pick up Maya. Since it is Friday afternoon, sundown is my deadline for emails.

Because, thank G-d, at sundown, in my family, we unplug.

Preparing for the Sabbath

Once the sun sets, we shut everything off: computers, cell phones, iPods, the television, the radio, everything. We don't answer the phone. We don't check voicemail. We don't even look at our to-do lists. We take a clean break from all the technology and all the pressure that is consuming our lives.

I've been unplugging from technology almost every Saturday for the last 25 years. It may seem counterintuitive, but observing this practice actually improves my connection to people. We don't call it our sanity ritual, but we could; like many others, we call it Sabbath. I've come to see keeping the Sabbath as a radical act.

I tell you my story with the hope that it will inspire you. I invite you to claim the Sabbath—this radical act of carving out time for you and your family—in whatever way works for you. I'm going to offer you the Jewish structures and rituals that go with "Shabbat" (the Hebrew word for Sabbath), but these practices can be adapted to any faith, agnostic, or secular tradition that you are comfortable with.

As one teacher I know says, "The Muslims have Friday, the Jews have Saturday, the Christians have Sunday, and so in the World-to-Come, we will all get a three-day weekend!" Indeed, this practice of taking a rest, one day in seven, is common to many of the world's ancient traditions, a lost wisdom that we need to reclaim.

You don't have to believe in G-d to observe the Sabbath. You don't have to be Jewish. You don't even have to like religion. Note the template and then make it yours. Do it on a Tuesday if you work on the weekends. It's not how you do it that matters, it's the act of taking a break—for 25 hours—that helps to make you whole.

What is Worthy, Endures

Shabbat is a practice that dates back somewhere between 2500 and 3500 years. Indeed, it's one of the Ten Commandments: "Honor the 7th day and keep it holy," the Old Testament advises. "For in six days G-d created the world, and on the 7th day G-d rested."

In my experience, this ancient idea—no matter what its origin—of taking one day out of seven off is brilliant. Although the tradition has been passed on for countless generations, we need it today more than ever.

Witness our lives of ever expanding to-do lists, electronic messages, and devices. Enough to put us on an exponentially accelerating trajectory of action, until we're moving at such an inhuman pace that we spin off into the ether. When do we get a break to come home to ourselves, our souls, our families? On Shabbat.

"No way," you say. "Not possible. I need to watch TV. I need to check my email. I don't have time to unplug."

I used to feel that way too. If you have never tried it, or if you tried it and you stopped, the idea of taking a day off every week seems impossible, even irresponsible. But if you weren't drawn to the idea of making some changes in your life, I'm guessing you wouldn't have read this far. Ever so respectfully, I'd like to ask you, "How well is it working for you and those you love now, when you don't take a break?"

The Dalai Lama invited a delegation of a dozen Rabbis to come visit him. Since the Chinese had made him and his people refugees from their homeland in Tibet, he wanted the Rabbis to answer the question, "How have you been able to sustain your tradition in 2000 years of exile from your land and your holy temples?" When one of the Rabbis spoke of the Shabbat practice, the Dalai Lama responded enthusiastically, "You mean you have a 25-hour meditation built into every week?"

Shabbat practices are not punitive prohibitions: "Thou shalt not text, thou shalt not email, and thou shalt not shop at the mall." Instead, they are an invitation to stop *doing*, so that you can simply *be* in enjoyment of the fruits of creation. They are a reminder of the radical concept that for this day everything is already perfect: There is nothing to do to improve it, being together is enough, and nothing needs tending that can't wait until tomorrow.

We breathe, we drink fresh water, we walk in the woods, we hug our children, we take time to listen to their questions, we take a nap, we dream, we share our dreams with each other. We live in the present. It is all good and there is nothing and no one to fix. Not even my husband, who won't clean the moldy food out of the fridge.

Letting Go

On a recent Friday night celebration, we welcomed the Shabbat with a big feast at a friend's home in Colorado. We were also celebrating my 50th birthday. Guests brought chocolate cake, pumpkin pie, an apple strudel, and mega chocolate chip cookies. Sam, all muscle and bone, who had eaten nothing but bread and butter for dinner, piled his plate high with a slice of each dessert and the largest cookie he could find. A nutrition-conscious mother looked at me, incredulous. With a none-too-subtle tone of judgment, she said, "You're going to let him eat all that sugar?"

"Here's how it goes in my house," I responded, paraphrasing the holy text: "Six days thou shalt discipline and mold thy children with all thy might, but the seventh day is the Sabbath and thou shalt give it a rest."

I get one day free of disciplining them. It's totally liberating. For all of us. As is the practice of letting go of my entire to-do list! Atlas holds the sky up by himself for the 25 hours once a week while I'm gone.

Our Family's Shabbat Rituals

Our family welcomes the Sabbath on Friday night after sundown with several rituals. I've done the same things more than a thousand times. But it doesn't feel repetitive. It feels grounding. Over time I've learned the power of adopting practices and doing them consistently. Some of the rituals are ancient and some our contemporary interpretation. Our family's intention is to capture the essence of the meaning of the rituals, not to follow them to the letter of the law.

Maya and Sam thrive on this repetition. During the week they live in a world that is constantly changing and moving too fast. "I love Shabbat!" Maya exclaims. The twins get our undivided focus and attention. Like cactus after fresh rain, they bloom. No matter what craziness is going on during the week, they can count on us to light candles, listen to what matters, and feast together on Friday night.

Most of the people we know don't eat dinner together as a family like we did when I was growing up. How can we these days, with both parents working, kids in a zillion extracurricular activities, evening meetings, the ever-present Internet and exponentially growing "smart" electronics? For us, the heart-to-heart and face-to-face come on Friday night and Saturday.

We begin the Sabbath with the following rituals on Friday:

Baking Bread: I mix the ingredients for Challah, the traditional Jewish braided egg bread, as soon as the kids are on the bus Friday morning, so the bread will have time to rise during the day (instructions on how to do this can be found at the end of this book).

But I practiced Shabbat weekly for about 15 years before I started making my own Challah. I just bought Challah at our local market. You don't have to bake homemade bread! But if you'd like to try , don't be intimidated. I am far from Suzy Homemaker. In fact, I have rarely baked a thing in my life.

I've found that there is something very satisfying about kneading the dough, creating something from scratch that will fill the house with a scrumptious aroma and fill our bellies with warm bread made with love. For those of us who make our living working on intangibles like "sustainability" or "social change" or even those who have more conventional steady jobs like selling real estate, teaching, counseling, or administrative work, there is very little that brings such immediate gratification of a job well done as baking fresh bread.

Winding Down: During the day at work, I know I'm heading towards the Shabbat sundown deadline. So I finish up whatever I can, and I communicate with colleagues on my progress. If something's not done, I commit to finishing it the following week. Same with returning calls from friends and tackling small "to dos" like making the kids' dentist appointments. I either complete them on Friday or make a plan for the following week. Because by sundown, it's all going to stop.

Tidying Our Space: We clean the house imperfectly on Friday afternoon. I'm already feeling overwhelmed by then, and housework is always at the bottom of my priority list, so this is no deep clean. But the mountain of school papers that have mysteriously multiplied since last Friday is reviewed and removed; the laundry is picked up off the floor, the dog's chewed stuffed animal remains go back to his cage, the dishes get put away, and the refrigerator experiments get a quick clean out. I know moms who scrub their houses from stem to stern before Shabbat. I admire them. But I accept my imperfections and the dog hair on the rug (if I don't have time to vacuum it). Still, the ritual of tidying helps our whole family. There is a semblance of order and calm that descends on our space. It soothes all our nerves.

Cooking for the Sabbath: I cook the one big meal I make each week. This does much to assuage my guilt that I'm not creating dinners worthy of Martha Stewart all week long. Our Shabbat dinners usually include big roast chickens plus greens, soup, salad, bread, veggies, and something sweet. I try to make these meals with love and abundance. I always make plenty of food. Often we host another family or a gaggle of guests. Though I sometimes get overwhelmed at the prospect of friends coming over, I inevitably enjoy them once they're here. And I love to feed them. The food I cook is enough to last for company and the next three meals, since when the sun goes down and the Sabbath begins, I'm resting and not cooking!

Wearing White: As sundown approaches, we change our clothes. Usually we all wear white. Joe, the kids, and I put on our whites or "Shabbat shirts" and look sharp. This simple act in itself has a kind of alchemical magic. We don't wear anything we've worn during the workweek, but instead adorn ourselves with jewels and scent our wrists with nice smells to evoke a regal feeling. For tonight we are Queens and Kings in our realm. White evokes purification and renewal. There have been many nights when I thought I was too exhausted to even enjoy the Sabbath meal. Then I donned my queenly costume (a lacy white top and a silky white skirt) and felt totally transformed and renewed. Try it sometime.

One Friday evening, Sam, who had just donned his white shirt, asked, "Mom, can I keep my pants on from school today?"

"Sure you can, if you want to, honey. I like to change everything 'cause it's like changing out of the costume I've worn at work all week and becoming a whole different character."

"I like that," said Sam emphatically. He ran to put on a fresh pair of pants. Don't you love it when your 9-year-old gets out of his sweat pants and dirty socks and puts on a tie because he wants to?

Making Music: We put on some rocking music for the occasion and dance and sing a little. The purpose of all this is to literally change our vibration, our resonance, our frequency, so we can open to a deeper level of renewal and healing.

Guitar playin' prayer

The Basics: Now come three essential Jewish rituals. There are more, but these are the basics:

1. Light the candles to bring in the light.

2. Share blessings over an overflowing cup of wine (with my grandmother's gold-rimmed plate under it to catch the drips) to offer gratitude for the abundance in our lives.

3. Bless and break that awesome bread together.

Lighting the Candles: Before lighting the candles we greet friends, chant, sing and drum together. The intention here is to build our connection to each other as well as a sense of awe and festivity in anticipation of the beginning of Sabbath time.

Toasting friends to celebrate the beginning of Shabbat.

Friends chatting

Welcoming guests with song

Drumming, singing, chanting before lighting candles

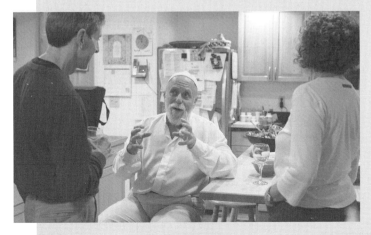

More friends chatting

During the candle lighting, we "send" the light to those in need of healing around the planet and to our loved ones far away, evoking a sense of connection. We recognize that this Shabbat gathering is for more than just us. After the blessings over the candles, in our home everybody hugs everybody—that includes any guests we have just met that evening. You might think that's too "touchy feely" for your crowd, but it melts hearts super quick. Now we're all in this together.

Candle lighting

Prayers over candle lightin

Old friends embracing. Feeling the love!

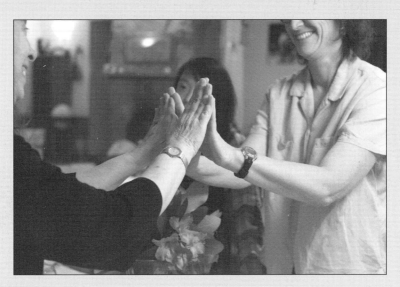

Friends

Blessing the Children: Next we bless the children. All the adults present find one or more kids, place their hands on their heads and say a spontaneous blessing. There is a traditional Hebrew prayer for this that roughly translates to, "May G-d bless you and protect you, shine G-d's light upon you, shower you with grace you and peace." We do a contemporary riff on this, blessing the kids to be the best human beings that they can be, with abundant health and strength and love and joy. It's a sweet moment and I think the kids really soak up these intentions: stand a little taller, breath a little deeper, feel the support and love of not only their own parents, but also the wider community.

Blessing over the children

Blessing the Wine and Voicing Gratitude: Then we say the blessing over wine or grape juice. We fill the cup to overflowing intentionally to signify all the goodness that is always present. And we go around the table, each one holding the cup and sharing out loud something we are grateful for from the week. You'd be surprised how the kids took to this from the time they could talk. They love having all eyes on them, with their faces glowing in the candlelight, while they describe what's good.

Ever notice that when we focus on the goodness in our lives and voice gratitude for it, our whole world-view shifts? Our heart rates and breathing settle, our muscles relax, our blood pressure goes down. You can practically feel endorphins flood your system when you take time to appreciate what you have. Everyone starts to smile. Despite the stress, despite the deadlines, despite the big concerns and small worries, life feels good. When we hear what others are grateful for, we feel grateful too. The mood is contagious. Suddenly we don't have to struggle, compete, crave; all we need is right here and right now.

Blessing over the wine gratitude for abundance in our lives

Still saying what we're grateful for one at a time.

Hand-washing: In case there's anything that's blocking us from receiving the gifts of the Sabbath eve, we have a remedy in— of course—another ritual. After the blessings over the candles and the wine, we wash our hands. We ask, "Is there anything we need to let go of from the week to become fully present to Shabbat time?" During which, to quote Rabbi Abraham Joshua Heschel, "The goal is not to have, but to be; not to own, but to share." One person pours water from a ceramic cup into a basin while another names (out loud or to him- or herself) what they need to let go of.

"I'm letting go of the emails I didn't get to and fatigue, fear, frustration," I say.

"I'm letting go of Miss Z yelling at me for cheering on my team at Gym," says Sam. He struggles with his Physical Education teacher. We do too. Miss Z gives Sam demerits for being too spirited. Go figure.

"I'm letting go of worrying about Ron and his mean dad." Maya's been the confidante of a gentle soul in her 4th grade class who tragically has a dad who beats him. "I'm worried about Ron," Maya reported to me at bedtime earlier in the week, "His family is nasty, but Ron wants me to fix it somehow and it's too much for me to take on. I'm only 9 years old!"

It's Joe's turn: "I'm letting go of all the emails I didn't get to and all the phone calls I didn't return and all the stuff on my to-do list that did not get done!"

The worries get washed away with the water. Someone else dries your hands. This simple gesture is to signify that there is nothing more you need to do today, but to receive. And you are loved.

Handwashing ceremony

Remarrying Every Week: My husband Joe and I have adopted another wonderful practice that we learned from Rabbis Arthur Waskow and Phyllis Berman of Philadelphia. We take our wedding rings off and re-marry each other. I place the ring on Joe's finger while he places my rings on mine. Then, with the same Hebrew phrase we shared under our wedding canopy, we lock eyes and each say to the other, "With this ring, you become sacred to me." Joe jokes that this is the AA approach to marriage, "one week at a time." When we do this, I'm often touched by a sweet feeling of renewal of love and an embodied reminder of the innocence and passion we felt on our wedding day long ago, before kids, wrinkles, and silver hair. It's good medicine.

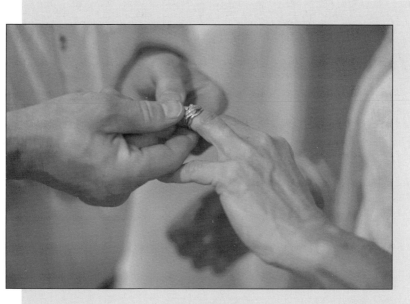

Remarriage every week

Blessing the hallah

Blessing the Bread: We do some more chanting and humming of tunes, and then it is time to break into the Challah that is warm from the oven. The kids remove its cover, and we all oooh and ahhh over the golden brown beauty. Then I lift the loaves with the invitation, "Everyone touch the bread or touch someone touching the bread," so once again we're all connected. After the blessing, we break chunks off with our hands and feed each other.

I'm reminded then of this story on the difference between heaven and hell. In hell there is a huge pot of rich stew. You are famished. But all you have is a super long spoon that reaches clear across to the other side of the pot. You are tantalized as you can reach the stew with your spoon, but you can't get it to your mouth. Everyone around the massive soup bowl is in the same situation and you all starve for eternity. In heaven: same stew, same spoons, same people. Only this time we all feed each other.

Enjoying the Feast: Now we get to dive into the meal, as all is blessed. Joe's the meat man in our family, so he carves the chicken. (I was vegetarian for 20 years until I got pregnant with twins and literally dreamed about roast beef sandwiches. Biology trumped ideology. Boy, was that steak good!) Having been baked covered for two hours, the meat falls right off the bone. We dig into chicken, onions, and sweet potatoes. The Challah is still so hot that the butter melts into it. We drink red wine, the kids have sweet grape juice (reserved only for Friday nights), and we usually have a side dish of something green. Our conversation is lively, sometimes humorous, sometimes political. Sometimes with the kids in the lead.

"Let's go around and appreciate what we love about Shabbat," Maya begins. "I'll go first. I love that we get to be together and you guys aren't on your Blackberries. Your turn, Sam."

"Shabbat is calming. I love that we don't have to do any homework or chores. That's the coolest."

Joe's next. "I like that I don't worry about emails or bills or what's not built yet in the barn. I like reading by the fire with you guys."

"I love not going anywhere," I confess. Far from town, we live in our cars during the week. "I love our Shabbat afternoon hikes. And I love chocolate for dessert!"

Tonight there is nothing to fix. Including the dishes. Though I'm usually pretty compulsive about making sure there's nothing piling up in the sink during the week—that's the one place I do like clean—on Friday night we don't do dishes. Because I usually do the cooking, Joe often will tackle the dishes Saturday evening.

Yummy food

Saturday Morning

"No chores, no shopping excursions, no emails, and no web surfing. What do you do?" you ask.

Here's what I don't do: I do not jump out of bed to shower, stretch, make lunches, sign homework papers, check Outlook for the day's schedule, make lists of what has to get done.

Here's what I do: I linger in bed reading last week's Sunday Styles section of the *New York Times*, or poetry, or *The Sun* magazine essays, or something else not about self-improvement. Sometimes I read Rabbi Shefa Gold's juicy translation of the Song of Songs or some other inspirational text of spiritual wisdom.

Then the kids come in for a snuggle. They are so happy to puppy pile between Joe and me. Even though they are exquisitely competent readers, they bring the book that we are reading aloud.

Later we get up and make Challah French toast out of last night's bread. I never make time to cook breakfast during the week so this in itself is a treat, especially with maple syrup from the maple trees on our property. Last spring Joe tapped 180 trees, collected 1800 gallons of sap, and boiled it down to 40 gallons of syrup. Yes, he is an industrious guy.

We lounge a bit more, grab the dog's leash, and head out for a family hike. This time it's Bear Mountain, across the street up a steep incline following a stream. The kids, at almost ten, are finally at the stage where they can beat us scrambling up the hill. At first they grumble about getting dressed and out the door, but once we're on the trail, they run ahead and compete over who's going to lead. It's huff and puff, heart-beating strenuous, but the reward is an expansive view to the west, overlooking rolling hills up into the Green Mountains of Vermont and the Berkshires in Massachusetts.

I recognize that you may not have the luxury of a mountain in your back yard, especially if you live in an urban area. Our friends Ben and Sally and their kids, Isaac and Molly, walk along the Charles River in Boston. Susan and Freddie stroll through Central Park in New York. The Israelis I know go to the beach and play Frisbee. You can walk anywhere, or ride your bikes, go for a swim, ski together as a family, or do just about any other outdoor activity. The key is being outside, and together.

As Winnie the Pooh famously said, "Christopher Robin didn't care what it was doing outside as long as he was out in it." In his book, *The Nature Principle*, Richard Louv (who coined the term "Nature Deficit Disorder") speaks of the power of nature to restore our spirits, mend our souls, and strengthen our bodies. More than a standard call to go for a walk in the woods, Louv says that our encounters with the natural world are essential to our humanity. He further argues that there is a direct correlation between the acceleration of our high-speed electronic era and our need to connect with nature: The more we are entwined with our electronic devices, the more we need to get outside to literally remember our humanity. So on Shabbat we let Mother Nature work her magic.

We hang out up at the top of Bear Mountain, with our eyes transfixed on that expansive view to the west. By now Maya, Sam, and Joe know I'm going to break into a Shabbat melody about a mountain with a view: "I lift up my eyes, to the great mountains." Thankfully, at this pre-teen age, the kids don't resist singing along. They're able to hold a tune now, so we can do harmonies. On the way back down, feeling good about having made it to the summit, we're relaxed. And since the pace is slow, the kids open up and tell us their more vulnerable secrets. Sam says, "Mom, I was annoyed when Connie took our pictures. Remember, to get us to laugh she asked, 'Whose room is the messiest? Who has the silliest jokes? Who's going to pitch for the Red Sox? Who is the kindest and the most compassionate?' You always answer Maya for compassionate and kind, and me for Red Sox pitcher. I'm not that young anymore, you know. I'm kind too." I never knew that my rough and tumble guy would want to be counted in the number of compassionate folks. Now I do. And I pay attention.

After the hike, we've worked up an appetite. We eat leftovers for lunch. Then it's time for one of my favorite weekly rituals: the Saturday afternoon Shabbat nap.

Saturday Afternoon

I'm not the kind of person who naps by nature. I'm a Type A, hurry-up, I'll-sleep-when-I'm-dead kind of mom. My dad was the founder and CEO of a fast-moving computer company. His unrelenting work ethic is practically embedded in my DNA. Take a break? Not in the program. But 25 years ago, while on a Kibbutz in Israel, where the afternoon snooze is a cultural given, I learned the power of napping. I wasn't able to practice it for years after our twins were born. But when they turned seven, we made them a deal: they could watch TV on Saturday afternoons—something that never happens during the week—so that we could get our nap.

The kids know my rules. "What are the 3 F's?" I ask. They respond in unison, "Fire, flood, or fatality." Unless it's one of those three, momma bear gets a Shabbat slumber undisturbed.

Sometimes Joe joins me or sometimes he plays guitar. In the Jewish tradition it is a double mitzvah (blessing) to make love on the Sabbath. One Rabbi I know says the braids of the Challah bread represent a man and a woman's intertwined bodies. When Joe joins me, and we're not dead tired from the week, we may get lucky. Other times it's all about a deep sleep.

After so many years of the Saturday afternoon nap, I think my body knows it's coming and is now almost hypnotically trained to go into a restorative sleep. I notice that when I don't get a nap on the Shabbat because I'm with relatives, or working, or at a party, I'm cranky for the following week.

I awake feeling like I've been on a week-long vacation. My mood is light, open, and grateful. It's during this time on Saturday afternoon, just before the sun sets, that the mystic Kabbalists say you reap the true harvest of Shabbat. Your soul is at its most open. Sometimes I have surprising insights, sometimes deeper conversations with friends or family who are present, sometimes just a sense of peace. All is well.

Shabbat Winds Down

Shabbat ends when the sun goes down. The tradition is to wait until we can see and count three stars in the sky—to be sure that the sun has truly set. The kids have fun going out to hunt for stars. Then we do a ritual of separation, marking the transition from Shabbat to the world of the week. We've learned it's important to put closure on this magnificent "palace in time," as Rabbi Abraham Joshua Heschel—a highly esteemed teacher, mystic, and prophetic voice from the early 20th century—poetically describes in his classic book, *The Sabbath*.

The purpose of Havdalah, the final Sabbath ritual, is to reap the harvest of our day, give thanks for it, and bring "the energy" of Shabbat into the week ahead of us. Havdalah (from the Hebrew word meaning "to differentiate") has three elements:

1. a braided candle

2. a glass of wine

3. a box of spices that delight the senses: nutmeg, cinnamon, cloves

Havdalah set. braided candle, spice box, wine cup

34

Our teacher, Rabbi Shefa Gold, says that the candlelight is about new insight; the wine represents what was intoxicating about our Shabbat; and the spices are symbolic of the sweet memories we want to take into the week.

We gather around the kitchen table and ask our children (and ourselves) aloud, "What was intoxicating, what insights, what sacred intentions do we want to bring into our week?"

"It was intoxicating soaking rays on the top of Bear Mountain and singing with you guys," Sam says.

Maya continues, "When we talked about the story of Jacob wrestling with the angel and then getting a blessing from him, I had some new ideas about how important it is to stick with hard things until they transform."

My sense from what Sam and Maya have shared, from the glow in their eyes, from their genuine listening to each other without interrupting and competing, from their arms wrapped around us, is that this is the medicine the kids need most from us to boost their immune systems, their self-esteem, their sense of peace and belonging in the world.

Joe reports, with a wink at me, "I want to bring in the happiness I felt in my nap with your momma."

I say, "The holiness I want to bring into the week is the love I feel for you guys and the peace that is in my heart right now." Somehow, by naming these things out loud and being witnessed in them, their power permeates the week.

Then we light the candle, and begin humming a tune together. We chant a prayer over the wine and then take a sip. As we're chanting the prayer for the spices, we pass the spice box around the circle and deeply inhale its scent. We say the prayer for the creation of light, holding our hands up to the light with fingers gently curled and playing with the shadows made there. This is a riff on the differentiation between day and night, just as we are now differentiating Sabbath from the rest of the week. Finally, and with dramatic flair, we douse the candle in the wine juice, immediately turn on the lights, and sing a song welcoming the new week: "Have a good week, a week of peace, may gladness reign and joy increase." Sometimes we'll take a moment to talk about something exciting or challenging coming up in the week ahead. Later that night, if I'm still awake after the kids are asleep, I take a moment for myself, step outside and imagine the week ahead and my Shabbat-inspired intentions for it. This is also good medicine.

Saturday Night

After Havdalah we often watch a movie or TV show together as a family. Recently we've been hooked on the TV series *Smash*, a fictional story about the making of a Broadway musical based on the life of Marilyn Monroe. The choreography, music, and lyrics are Broadway-quality, - so it's fun to watch (if a bit racy for the kids sometimes with the skin-to-skin contact; that's when I follow my own mother's lead from when I was little and firmly cover their eyes, one hand for each kid.) Watching movies or TV shows together is fun, but what the movies are about is not really the point. What really matters is the family time spent snuggling on the couch, and our transitioning together back into the plugged-in world.

Last week, for a change of pace, we went to our local coffee house, where Charles Neville was playing saxophone along with a couple of prodigies—one is the 26-year-old son of good friends, a young man I've known since he was seven; the other is a stellar 28-year-old jazz diva vocalist of Billie Holiday quality. Tired from the Bear Mountain climb, the twins started to fade. Sam had his head on my right knee, Maya on my left. Could there be a more perfect moment? During the week, no doubt, I'd miss appreciating the feel of my children leaning against me, focused as I usually am on my mile-long to-do list, trying not to drop any balls. But that night I fully received how sweet it is.

And The Week Begins Again

By Sunday morning the 136 emails in the inbox don't bug me—I know I'll take care of them on Monday. The deficit in the finance meeting we had last week looms less large. We've always been blessed with enough. The thing about Joe that was gnawing at me on Friday—how he never remembers to write down the names of my friends who call—isn't bothering me anymore and doesn't seem worth talking about. Neither does the fact that he doesn't see the "science experiments" in the fridge. After all, Joe is the guy who goes to the recycling and trash dump in our town every Tuesday. He's the breakfast-making dad too. Now that I've experienced such a peaceful day, I find that I appreciate him for what he does do and feel no need to find fault with what he doesn't.

The purple rug may never be free of its bright yellow dog hair, the kids may not learn to put their stuff away until college. I can't volunteer at Sam's book fair this year. My tribute to my dad may not be perfect prose. But none of that matters. What matters is enjoying my family, having fun at work, doing the best I can without judging myself or anyone else, taking care of myself, nurturing my marriage, getting outside, and being grateful for the gift of this awesome planet.

This is how the Shabbat consciousness permeates the week. Each week by observing the Sabbath I learn again that the world will still turn without me holding it up, that I am allowed to let go, that I can be less hard on myself. During the week, when my Type A, hard-driving self is back full tilt, the peace I felt on the previous Sabbath reminds me that it's okay to go for a swim in the morning, take a few minutes after the kids are safely on the school bus to make my favorite blueberry smoothie, and to step outside to actually smell the lilacs before I jump on the computer.

Renewed by a day of rest, I remember again that if I respond to emails 30 minutes—or even a day—later than usual, my colleagues will still love me. Indeed, people who have worked with me over the years know this rhythm and respect it. If you want to get Sara, it's by sundown Friday or you'll hear from her next week. One long-term business partner even reported that he felt more at ease himself, just knowing that Joe and I were practicing Sabbath. The world does not come to an end. As the poet Robert Bly says, I find that "if I lay down, no one will die."

A Reality Check:
Living in 21ˢᵗ-Century America

All the pressures of our fast-paced, work-oriented, plugged-in culture work against any of us practicing Shabbat. Despite our best intentions, reality—and hard choices—often kick in.

Maybe you want to observe the Sabbath, but you can't find the time. Your family life is too busy. The kids have sports on Saturday mornings. Sunday, there are birthday parties to attend and homework assignments to finish. What do you do about Saturday morning soccer?

You can still practice Shabbat sometimes, or for half a day, or on Sunday one week instead of Saturday. It will never feel perfect exactly, and other activities might get in the way. Does that mean you can't do it at all? Or that it's somehow not okay? No!

We don't want Shabbat to feel punitive. We, too, participate in the culture at large. So we make choices. For us, Friday night is pretty sacred—we almost never miss it. When Sam's baseball coach asked if we could do a make-up game for a rain-out on Friday night, we politely said no. But we went to the game on Saturday. When our Saturdays get filled with other activities and we don't have that family cocoon time, we aim to do those activities with "Shabbat Consciousness." We try to go with the flow. We don't use our phones or bring our iPads to the sidelines. We enjoy the sun and the easy banter with other parents and choose not to have another agenda for the moment.

At the same time, we've all come to value Shabbat's restorative powers. When Maya's swim coach said kids could come to practice on Saturday or Sunday or both, Maya said, "Mom, I need my Saturday mornings to just be. I'll go on Sunday, OK?"

And Sam, to my great surprise, opted out of ice hockey last year because the early morning Saturday practices interfered with Shabbat snuggle time. Still, his best sports buddy is cheering for him to join the team, so he may make a different choice next winter.

We aim for progress, not perfection. As our teacher Rabbi Nadya Gross wisely shares, "Expecting perfection of ourselves is the highest form of self-abuse."

Try having a Sabbath feast one Friday night this month (there are detailed instructions at the end of this book for what you need to get started) and see what the impact is. Maybe you'll be like my friend Marianne, who told me, "George and I did a whole 25-hour Shabbat like you encouraged us to do for the first time last week, and we felt like we'd been on vacation for a month. We love it!"

Think of the Shabbat practice on a spectrum. On one end is perfect rest: You don't drive anywhere, buy anything, spend any time with a screen in front of your eyes; you just hang out and be for 25 hours. We get that day about a half dozen times per year. On the other end is no rest—a day like any other, where you are going full tilt, nonstop, from waking up till your head crashes on the pillow 18 bleary-eyed hours later. Start your Shabbat practice somewhere in between. Build it up slowly. Notice the impact on you and your family. And by all means, don't worry if you don't get it right. Because of my increasing delight with the experience, my practice has slowly grown over the years to include most of the 25 hours of Shabbat, on most Saturdays of the year (except during baseball season). But I started with just Friday night.

For some families it's hard to dissolve the tension and anger that have built up during the week. "What about when you just can't let go of a week's worth of stress and resentment by the time the sun sets on a Friday night?" a friend asks. "Aren't you ever just so pissed off at Joe that you don't want to let him off the hook?"

I will come clean and admit that I have a pretty decent zero-to-sixty acceleration rate when it comes to getting mad at my husband. I can convince myself of the righteousness of my stories of how I'm innocent and he's guilty. But it's exactly because of this tendency that the Shabbat discipline of letting go is so powerful.

One Friday night I was furious with Joe. I thought he was being angry, reactive, and unappreciative. I'd asked him to come help me set up a table for guests who would be arriving soon, and he yelled, "Quit bugging me; can't you see I'm working here!"

"Like I'm not!" I yelled back. This was the tickertape in my head: "You ungrateful bastard. Do you know what I do every day for you and the kids and work and the schools? No, you don't have a clue!" My internal prosecuting attorney was off like a steamroller, and Joe was guilty in my personal court of law.

But I had to shut down that steam engine. It was almost sundown and—according to my inner Shabbat compass—I didn't have a choice. So I stopped setting the table, went down the hill to the stream outside our house, knelt by the bubbling water, and prayed for compassion and letting go. I began to chant a song from our wedding. I breathed. I asked for help. I took my time. And by the time I ascended the path again and came in the door, I was looking at him with different eyes, a different heart perhaps.

"I don't want to go into Shabbat bitching at each other," I said, my tone softened, my hand on his heart. "Let's do it differently."

And we did. By the time we got to the hand-washing, we were truly ready to "get married" again. This time we were even a little more grateful than usual.

On any other day I might have let my anger escalate until we were in full-blown conflict. I would steam, Joe would steam, we would both be convinced we were right, and the fabric of our marriage would erode a little more. But on Shabbat we do it differently. We have an agreement not to try to fix each other. And it makes a real difference in the quality of our relationship. I'm not sure we would have made it this far—19 years strong and still loving each other—without our weekly practice of rest. I don't know how any other couple does without it.

Not Born to Buy

One of my favorite things about Shabbat is that during the 25 hours my family and I spend observing Shabbat each week, we learn how satisfying it is not to buy anything. The traditional Shabbat approach is not to engage in any commerce, not because that would be evil, but because, given the perfection of creation in the moment, there is nothing we need to acquire. On our best Sabbaths, we take a day off from shopping for food, clothes, books, toys, vacation items, electronics, or sports gear. We take a day off from hearing or seeing advertisements that remind us of all the things we just *have* to have. We take a day off from spending any money at all. We don't get in the car to drive to the mall.

After I observe Shabbat, I find I have less desire to buy stuff just for the sake of filling an unnamed hunger. I learn each week that the best way to feed that hunger is through connection with myself, my soul, my friends, my family, G-d, and the great healer, Mother Earth herself. I discover anew how satisfying it is not to buy anything.

Like an addict going cold turkey, you'll experience some withdrawal symptoms at first. In the beginning, you'll need a lot of self-discipline to move beyond your habitual patterns. But once you get through that phase, you're free. As you adjust to a new pattern, you learn to slow down and pay attention. Everything looks, feels, and even tastes different.

A deep peace spreads within, around, and through you—a peace that's a salve to your nerves and a balm to your soul. The desire for stuff, the anger, the disappointment, the blame, the bad feelings, everything, just . . . dissolves.

We all sometimes feel that the pace of our lives is unsustainable. We are all hungry for a break. What I've learned and am blessed by in practicing Shabbat is that I am more grateful and relaxed all week, our children are growing up happy and resilient, and my relationship with Joe "re-boots" from one long to-do list back to a loving relationship. As an added bonus, our credit card debt—and the stress that goes with it—has gone down because we're buying less stuff. and when we stay home and don't burn any gas, that's one small step for the climate. Imagine the implications if we all did this: a day every week for the Earth to restore the balance.

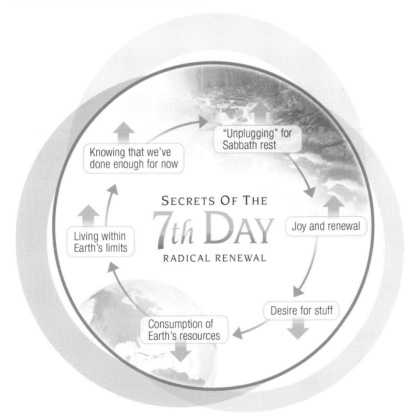

These are the Secrets of the 7th day: radical renewal from the inside out, for you and me, our families, our communities, and the one and only awesome planet that we all call home.

Tracing the arrows, beginning with "unplugging for Sabbath rest," you can read the picture above as follows: When we unplug for Sabbath rest, our sense of joy and renewal increases, which causes our desire for stuff to decrease. That's a win for the planet, as our consumption of Earth's resources also decreases. Now we are increasingly living within Earth's limits, a boon for sustainability the world over. And when we live within Earth's limits, we begin to accept and even revel in our own limits. We are Earthlings, after all. We've done enough for now. And so it's time to unplug for Shabbat again. The cycle renews itself, growing stronger and deeper each time.

Sara's Guidelines for Radical Renewal on the 7th Day

A big shift in my thinking about Shabbat came when a big-hearted neighbor I met at a local concert one Saturday night said, "Hi, you're new in town, right? Come to my house next Friday night for Shabbat!"

"I'd love to," I replied, truly delighted to be invited. "But how did you know I am Jewish?"

"I didn't," she said. "I invite everybody!"

Find a friend to do this with—whether your friend knows the practice or not. Having a buddy helps. To start, take one evening off from all electronics and screens to be with your family in a different way. See how it works for you. Keep the following tips in mind:

1. There is no one "right" way to practice Shabbat: Whatever you do is enough, and just what you should be doing.

2. Start small: Just lighting one candle is enough (see #1); you can gradually add more rituals, if you want to. When I first began observing the Sabbath, I only lit candles on Friday night when friends were with me. Later, I added the wine and would have Challah only if there was a store in town where I could buy it. Gradually, I took on more of the practice.

3. Spend time in nature: Just get outside. It's an instant mood lifter. Being outdoors helps us reconnect to the Earth and to our families; time in nature is healing. You can be a city dweller and still be in nature. Spend the day in Central Park in New York City, stroll down the banks of the Charles River in Boston, head

to the shores of Lake Michigan in Chicago, or soak up rays on the beach in L.A.

4. Shabbat works even for the stressed: Remember how crazy my life was on Friday afternoon? I get stressed, reactive, and short-tempered like everyone else. I'm no saint. All the more reason for the Shabbat soul balm. You don't have to be in a good or spiritual place or even believe in G-d to observe Shabbat. You'll still benefit just as much. Maybe even more.

5. Having the intention is enough: There is no perfection here, just the intention to rest, renew, celebrate, and be grateful. Setting the intention to take a break from our daily routine in order to just "be" and setting aside some time to allow that to happen are what matters. Over time your practice will grow.

Getting Started:
Sara's Shabbat at a Glance

Materials for welcoming the Sabbath on Friday night:

1. Challah: You can buy this bread at most grocery chains or local bakeries. Or, if you're inspired, make it yourself. See my recipe for the challenged homemaker below.

2. A nice cloth napkin to cover the Challah or an embroidered Challah cover

3. Red wine for the adults and grape juice or sparkling cider for the kids

4. A special wine goblet or nice glass (for the abovementioned wine/juice)

5. Two white candles, candlesticks, and matches

6. White tablecloth

7. A hand-washing cup, basin, and clean hand towel

Materials for saying farewell to the Sabbath on Saturday night:

1. Braided candle: you can buy one on-line or at Judaica stores.

2. Something to hold spices; this could be a small glass bowl, a wooden box, or a nutmeg shaker. If you score a Havdalah kit—which I got as a present after ten years of practicing without one—a spice box is included. Fill your box with aromatic spices: nutmeg and cloves are excellent choices.

3. A glass of wine

Setting the Shabbat Table

The Friday night meal is the one time in the week that I try to set the table as the aesthetic designer that I'm not. Fresh flowers are great. (The kids can go outside and pick them from your yard. They will also like making place cards for guests, if you are looking for an activity to keep them busy as you prepare.) Set the table with a white tablecloth and cloth napkins, if you have them, and use your best dishes. I took my daughter to my mother's house recently, and we packed up my grandmother's china that I used to eat on as a child. Maya always chooses to set the table on Friday nights with these dishes now. We all like the idea that we are eating off the same plates that have been used in my family for four generations.

Setting the table

The set table should include these items:

• two candlesticks with white candles

• Challah covered with a cloth napkin

• one wine goblet with red wine poured to the brim and spilling over to the saucer below it

• hand-washing cup, basin, and hand towel

• flowers or something green from outside

Sara's Scrumptious Challah Bread Recipe

(With a bow to Andi Waisman and Elana Klugman, who passed it along to me)

8 Ingredients:

1 tablespoon yeast

10 cups flour (we use 8 white, 2 whole wheat)

2 cups water

¼ cup canola oil

½ cup honey or maple syrup

1 tablespoon salt

4 eggs

poppy seeds and/or toasted sesame seeds

The Dough: Start before noon. Take two cups of warm water, add a tablespoon of yeast and let the mixture sit for 10 minutes.

During that time, mix ¼ cup canola oil and ½ cup of honey or real maple syrup. Take out a large bowl and beat 3 eggs and one tablespoon of salt. When ten minutes are up, inhale the aroma of the yeasty water and the honey (or maple syrup) mix (it's good medicine); then pour all these together into the large bowl and beat for a minute or so. Now start adding the flour, one cup at a time. For the first few cups, you can stir the mixture with a spoon. Eventually, though, you'll have to get your hands in there. For newcomers to challah baking, the question is,"when have I added enough flour?" The short answer is, "When it is stretchy; moist but not so moist that you won't be able to braid it later."

Kneading the Dough:

Kneading is great therapy! With bent elbows, place hands on top of dough and press with enthusiasm until your elbows are straight. Fold the dough and repeat. Knead for fifteen minutes or so (if you're in a hurry, ten will work), pouring your love into it. (I mean it: Maya says that's what makes it taste so good.) I often think about the week that was and the things I'm grateful for as

I work the dough. Good prep for the gratitude to come at sundown, and it shifts my mood for a moment away from the hectic day ahead. When done, the dough should be moist, but not wet, and form a large oval.

Letting the Dough Rise: Take some canola oil and spread it over the dough to keep it from getting dry while rising. Cover with a cloth and let it rise somewhere warmish (I put mine on top of the fridge) for 3 or more hours. After that first rise, take both hands and punch down the dough. Air bubbles fly out. This is fun, and the kids love to do it if they're home from school in time. Knead for a while, cover again, and let rise in a warm place for about another hour. Repeat punching down.

Now it's time to braid: My kids have been doing this since they were three years old, so by now they're pros. Take the dough and divide it into thirds (if you want three Challahs) or fourths (if you want four.) Divide each mound of dough into three strands. Then braid each strand into a loaf. If you don't know how to braid, find a 9-year-old girl to show you. Crack and beat an egg and then "paint" each loaf (another thing kids love) with the egg . Shake some toasted sesame seeds or poppy seeds on top. They'll stick to the egg.

Preheat oven to 350° and bake for about 25 minutes. Top should be golden brown when done. If you turn the bread over and tap the loaf, it should sound hollow. Remove the bread from the oven, cover it, place it on the table, and get ready for the culinary highlight of the week.

Braiding hallah bread

Hallah braided

"Washing" the hallah with egg

Sara's Shabbat Chicken

2 roasting chickens
10 cloves of garlic
2 onions
2 lemons
olive oil
tamari soy sauce
salt
pepper
rosemeary

Acquire a covered roasting pan from your mother, a friend, a yard sale, or Ebay. Preheat oven to 425°. Wash two chickens, pat dry, and place in pan. Cut four ¼ inch slices in each chicken, two by legs, two on breasts. Place a clove of garlic inside each of those slices and one in the cavity of each chicken (ten cloves total). Slice two onions, and place half the onions inside the chicken cavities and the rest somewhere in the pan. Cut two lemons in half. Squeeze one lemon half over each chicken. Place the remaining lemon halves inside the chicken cavities. Splash some olive oil and some tamari soy sauce over the chickens (I never measure this stuff). Add salt, pepper, and rosemary and you're done. Then, for good measure, cut a bunch of sweet potatoes in half, and place them in the pan around the onions. Change the temperature to 350°. Bake for 2 hours. Voilà! Even my soul-foodie friend Marsia says this is the best chicken she's ever tasted made by a white girl.

Sara's Crispy Potatoes

4 potatoes
olive oil
salt

This is super simple and always a hit. Scrub potatoes. Cut each potato in half lengthwise, and then cut each half into wedges (about 8 wedges per potato). Spread a little olive oil on bottom of a baking dish. Now coat the potatoes with olive oil and a generous amount of salt to taste. Bake at 425° for 20 minutes, then at 350° for about another 30 minutes. This makes them super crispy on the outside and melt-in-your-mouth soft on the inside.

Green Leafy Veggies

2 heads kale, collards or Swiss chard
2 tablespoons sesame oil
2 teaspoons tamari soy sauce, (or more, to taste)
1 large lemon

Steam green leafy veggies until they are "al dente"—not over-cooked—which takes from 10–20 minutes, depending on the greens. In a serving bowl, mix 2 tablespoons of sesame oil (more or less—my editor for this manuscript says I have to give you exact amounts, but I never season things exactly), 2 teaspoons of tamari (same give or take concept on measurement here), and the juice of one lemon. After you've made this a few times, you'll have a sense of how much lemon, tamari, and oil to use. Add steamed greens to the bowl and mix until the greens are coated with the sauce. Enjoy!

Blueberry Smoothies for Dessert

2 cups frozen blueberries
1 frozen banana
1 scant cup apple juice or milk
ice cubes

Place ingredients in a blender, and blend on high for a totally healthy, yummy frozen dessert, adding more liquid if necessary (the less you use, the more likely your kids will think it's ice cream).

Sara Version of the Sabbath Prayers

Here are the Hebrew transliterations and my English translations (with a bit of poetic license) of the Sabbath prayers. Use these if you like, or make up your own. We chant the prayers; other families sing them. There are lots of different tunes. Off-key is fine! You can find tunes to these on-line by Googling "Jewish Sabbath Prayer Melodies." Listen to a few to see which melodies move you. These prayers have been around for thousands of years and have been sung in languages all over the world, so there is lots of variation. Or make up your own melodies! That is very much in line with the tradition—in every generation new melodies are born.

Over the light (light the candles as you sing):

Baruch Ata Adonai, Elohenu Melech HaOlam, Asher Kidshanu b'Mitzvah Tov, V'Tzivanu L'Hadlik Nair, Shel Shabbat.

Blessed are You, Source of All, who commands us to light the lights of Shabbat. (And then I add, "May our hearts and homes be filled with light.")

Over the wine (hold up the goblet as you sing):

Baruch Ata Adonai, Elohenu Melech HaOlam, Boree Pri Ha Gafen.

Blessed are You, Source of All, who creates the fruit of the vine.

Over the hand-washing:

Fill a large ceramic cup or small pitcher—your most aesthetically pleasing one—with warm water. Have a basin and a dry cloth next to it. Ideally, there are three people participating: one person to pour the water, one to have his or her hands washed, and one to dry that person's hands. We go around the table until everyone has had a chance to wash, pour, and dry.

Baruch Ata Adonai, Elohenu Melech HaOlam, Asher Kidshanu b'Mitzvah Tov, V'Tzivanu al NaTilat Ya'Da-eem.

Blessed are You, Source of All, who commands us to lift up our hands in service.

Over the Challah:

We always bless the bread last. You can remember this because it is covered, waiting for its turn! With great dramatic effect, saying "1 . . . 2 . . . 3," we have the youngest folks around the table pull the cloth off the Challah in unison. It is usually still steaming hot—heat your store-bought loaf in the oven as you set the table so it will be hot too—and we all literally go, "Oooo, Ahhh." Then, while lifting up the Challah, one of us says, "Now touch the Challah or touch someone else who is touching the Challah so we are all connected." Once we're connected, we sing the prayer together.

Baruch Ata Adonai, Elohenu Melech HaOlam, Ha Motzi Lechem Min Ha'Aretz.

Blessed are You, Source of All, who brings forth bread from the Earth.

Break off hunks of the bread and feed each other. Time to feast!

Appendix

The Order of Things: My friend Stephanie Ryan, one of the early enthusiastic readers and practitioners of the *Secrets of the 7th Day* said, "Sara, I need the flow of the day all in one place for reference. It's going to get tacked onto the frig." This is for you Steph:

Fri AM:

Purchase or bake Hallah sometime today. Also pick up whatever food you want for Fri feast and Saturday as you won't be cooking or shopping Saturday!

Friday Afternoon:

House beauty and order. (to extent you feel like picking up!)

Feast prep, table set

Change to shabbes finery attire. (white if that feels right to you)

Sundown:

Song and dance as spirit moves you throughout

Candle lighting

Welcome the angels (angel cards if you have)

Blessing over wine

Hand washing letting go ritual

Blessing over bread

Feast

Gratitudes for the meal at end of feast.

Saturday AM:

Sleep in!

Read, rest, stretch enjoy slow morning

Family get together—what do you want to have happen today?

Some time outdoors together

Saturday Afternoon:

Lunch together—bless grape juice or wine and break bread again.

Freedom

Afternoon nap

Time before sunset is sweet to soak the gifts of the day.

Sunset plus three stars Havdalah ritual to welcome back the week

Sat night party of your choice. (Family movie, games, night out, whatever.)

Whallah!

Acknowledgements and Gratitude

Ultimately, Shabbat is about cultivating gratitude. I am grateful beyond measure for so many souls who have guided me on this path. My holy teachers, Rabbis Shefa Gold, Nadya Gross, and Sheila Weinberg. Andi Waisman, who introduced me to our soulful Shabbat practice when she spotted me at that coffee house 22 years ago and invited me over for Friday night. My spirit buddy for life, Ariel Lippman, and all my KZ and Wisdom School brothers and sisters. To Linda Booth Sweeney, my dear friend and colleague, who provided the spark for this book when she proclaimed, "Sara, you have to teach us how to do Shabbat, we're all desperate for a break in our lives!" To my women's circle of 18 years, for getting me through everything and to my spiritual huskies of the heart, who romp with me outdoors in all weather. Thanks to Margaret Metzger of blessed memory, who taught a 15-year-old, "I know what I feel when I see what I write." Thanks also to Patricia Lee Lewis and Mara Bright, my writing inspirations and midwives. To Jennifer Margulis, inspiration and editor beyond compare and to my publishing team at White Cloud Press, Steve Scholl and Christy Collins for believing in the message in this book and for bringing it to fruition with expertise and style. Thanks too to my "queen of logistics" the generous and miraculous Mira Nussbaum.

Most of all, my deepest gratitude to my soul mate Joe Laur and to the two beautiful and brilliant lights in my life, our children Sam and Maya who share Shabbat with me every week and bless me with so much love.

About the Author

Sara Schley is the founder and president of Seed Systems, an international consulting company dedicated to accelerating our transformation of this planet to a world where all life thrives. Sara has worked for over two decades in multi-national business, non-profit, government, and academic sectors; creating, designing, facilitating, teaching, and coaching leadership programs and cultural change initiatives for a sustainable world.

Sara's most recent creation, along with her stellar partners, is *River Story: Sustainability from the Inside Out.* Sara is the co-author of *The Necessary Revolution: How Individuals and Organizations are Working Together to Create a Sustainable World* and *Learning for Sustainability.* Sara lives in rural Western Massachusetts, where she shares her home, heart, and Shabbat with her husband Joe Laur, children Maya and Sam, and their love dog Simba. Find out more about Sara and Sabbath reflections and activities at Secretsof7thday.com. And find more of Sara's professional work integrating sustainability from the inside out at seedsystems.net.

About the Photographer

Marsia Shuron Harris/aka Mother Turtle is a singer, songwriter, photographer and founder of Healing the Stories We Tell Ourselves, a unique interactive personal enrichment experience that helps to shift the toxic stories that we are carrying about ourselves and others. She lives in Western Massachusetts amongst the forest, where she draws her inspiration from the beauty of the natural world that surrounds her. Find her online at www.MotherTurtle.com